JUST A TOUCH
of MAGIC

Written by Mary Hathaway
Illustrated by Jan Nesbitt

Collins Educational
An Imprint of HarperCollinsPublishers

Once there was a princess who wanted a very special Christmas present. She wanted something beautiful, very beautiful, with just a touch of magic.

Everyone tried very hard to please the princess.

The Duke of Montigum bought the princess a horse. Horses were beautiful to him, and he didn't know anything about magic.

"It's lovely," said the princess, "and brown is my favourite colour... for horses," she added politely. But it was not her idea of something beautiful, very beautiful, with just a touch of magic.

She ordered the horse to be taken away and trained to give rides to children in the palace gardens during the summer.

The Countess of Arabon brought the princess an enormous crown made of pink sugar and filled with chocolates. It was certainly magic, for whichever chocolate you chose, it always had your favourite centre.

"It's a lovely present," said the princess, "and I'm very fond of chocolates," she added politely. But it was not her idea of something beautiful, very beautiful, with just a touch of magic.

She ordered the crown to be taken away and divided up amongst the poorest children in the city.

The Court Magician gave the princess a special plant which, he said, grew strawberry ice-creams. But the Court Magician had muddled up his spells. The plant sprouted mustard sandwiches instead.

"It's lovely," said the princess, "and I'm sure mustard sandwiches can be very tasty," she added politely. But it was not her idea of something beautiful, very beautiful, with just a touch of magic.

She ordered the special plant to be put in the palace greenhouse. She thought that even the poorest children in the city wouldn't want mustard sandwiches!

Now, far away in the lonely wastelands of the north there lived a queen whose fingers twinkled with magic. While she was riding through a snowstorm, a snowflake brushed against her little finger. Touched with magic, the snowflake grew larger and became as hard as diamonds but still as light as thistledown.

The queen rode on but the wind swirled the snowflake into a wild dance, away and away into the frozen darkness. It danced the snowflake right out of the lonely wastelands and into the city.

The wind carried the snowflake through the narrow streets until it came to rest at the feet of a small, ragged boy who was sitting on a step eating some of the princess's chocolates. There it shone and sparkled and made a pool of light on the ground.

"Oh, you are beautiful, so beautiful," said the small boy. "You are a gift fit for the princess."

He picked the snowflake up carefully and climbed the hill to the palace. There he gave it to a footman, who placed it on a velvet cushion and told him to take it to the princess.

"The princess won't like that as much as my beautiful horse!" said the Duke of Montigum, as he saw it being carried across the courtyard.

"The princess won't like that as much as my sugar crown filled with magic chocolates!" said the Countess of Arabon, as it was taken through the hall.

"The princess won't like that as much as my special plant!" said the Court Magician, as it passed up the stairs.

The snowflake shone and sparkled and made a little pool of light on the cushion. When the princess saw it she laughed with delight. "The snowflake is as hard as diamonds and as light as thistledown," she said. "This is my very special Christmas present."

At last, at last she had something beautiful, very beautiful, with just a touch of magic.